Dodge Is Ready to Play!

By Sally Cowan

One day, Dodge the kitten caused lots of problems at home.

Grace made some oatmeal for breakfast, and Dodge leapt up on the bench to try it!

That's my breakfast, Dodge!
Oatmeal is not healthy for kittens!

Then Dodge laid down and rested his head on Mum's soft work jacket.

He spread black fur all over the jacket!

Mum was getting ready to go to work.
Now she would be late!

Dad left his laptop open on the desk and headed into the kitchen to get a snack.

Dodge stepped on the laptop and messed up Dad's work!

Dad waved Dodge out of the way.

The kitten leapt out of the open window.

Grace had dug a tunnel in the sand pit for her toy train.

An insect was fluttering above the tunnel.

Dodge spotted the insect and took a big breath ...

He pounced on the insect, and the tunnel caved in!

"Dodge!" cried Grace.
"You are too heavy for my tunnel!"

Play with this tennis ball instead, Dodge!
Ready? Go!

Grace threw the ball for Dodge, but Dodge spotted another insect.

A bright red ladybird flitted around a cactus plant.

Dodge jumped up to catch it!

Grace watched on with dread as the silly kitten hit the cactus plant.

Then Dodge had a **big** problem – a cactus spike got stuck in his cheek!
It was not pleasant.

Dad had to pull the spike out.

"Hold steady, Dodge," said Dad.

Dodge needed a nap after his big fright!

Grace spread out a blanket on Dodge's bed and patted him.

"You never meant to cause all those problems, did you, Dodge?" she said.

CHECKING FOR MEANING

1. What happened to Mum's work jacket? *(Literal)*
2. What did Dodge do to Grace's tunnel? *(Literal)*
3. Why do you think Grace threw the tennis ball for Dodge? *(Inferential)*
4. Do you think Grace was right to forgive Dodge for causing all those problems? Why? *(Evaluative)*

EXTENDING VOCABULARY

breakfast	Read the word *breakfast*. How many sounds are in this word? What are they? What are some breakfast foods?
leapt	What is the base word for *leapt*? What did Dodge do when he leapt? What is another word the author could have used instead of *leapt*?
dread	How are you feeling if you feel dread?

MOVING BEYOND THE TEXT

1. Have you ever had a cheeky pet? What did they do?
2. What are some things you could do to keep a kitten out of trouble?
3. What do kittens eat? What shouldn't they eat?
4. If you had a kitten like Dodge, what would you name it? Why?

TIME TO WRITE

Imagine it is the day after the story ended. Write about what Dodge gets up to on that day. Does he cause any more problems?